Let's Get C

BRUNCH

Over **100** delicious dishes

igloobooks

igloobooks

Published in 2017
by Igloo Books Ltd
Cottage Farm
Sywell
NN6 0BJ
www.igloobooks.com

Designed by Nicholas Gage
Edited by Bobby Newlyn-Jones

Food photography and recipe development
© Stockfood, The Food Media Agency
Additional imagery © iStock / Getty Images
Cover images: © iStock / Getty Images

LEO002 0417
2 4 6 8 10 9 7 5 3 1
ISBN 978-1-78670-860-1

Printed and manufactured in China

Contents

Meat Dishes

Tomato and Bacon Open Sandwich

4 rashers smoked streaky bacon
2 slices sourdough bread
2 tomatoes
½ clove garlic
2 tbsp olive oil
handful of rocket (arugula) leaves

1. Preheat the grill to its highest setting.
2. Grill the bacon and sourdough for 3 minutes on each side or until the bread is toasted and the bacon is crisp.
3. Meanwhile, cut the tomatoes in half then scrape out and discard the seeds.
4. Cut the tomato flesh into strips.
5. When the bread is ready, rub it with garlic and drizzle with olive oil then arrange the bacon, tomatoes and rocket on top.

Prosciutto-wrapped Halloumi Kebabs

300 g / 10 ½ oz / 2 ½ cup Halloumi, cubed
150 g / 5 ½ oz / 1 cup prosciutto
28 cherry tomatoes
2 shallots, quartered
12 bay leaves, halved

1. Put 12 wooden skewers in a bowl of water and leave to soak for 20 minutes.
2. Preheat the grill to its highest setting.
3. Wrap each Halloumi cube in prosciutto then thread them onto the skewers with the tomatoes, shallots and bay leaves.
4. Grill the kebabs for 4 minutes on each side or until they are golden brown and cooked through.

SERVES: **2** | PREP TIME: **10 MINS** | COOKING TIME: **12 MINS**

Steak with Garlic Sauce and Parsnip Chips

2 skirt steaks
1 tbsp olive oil

FOR THE SAUCE
1 tbsp butter
2 cloves garlic, finely chopped
½ tsp cracked black peppercorns
1 tbsp brandy
200 ml / 7 fl. oz / ¾ cup double cream

FOR THE PARSNIP CHIPS
3 parsnips, cut into long chips
2–3 litres / 3 ½ pints–5 pints / 8–12 cups sunflower oil

1. Heat the oil in a deep fat fryer, according to the manufacturer's instructions, to a temperature of 130°C. Fry the parsnips for 10 minutes without browning.
2. Brush the steaks with oil and season. Fry in a smoking hot frying pan for 2 minutes on each side. Transfer the steaks to a warm plate, wrapped in a double layer of foil.
3. Pull up the fryer basket and increase the temperature to 190°C. Cook the chips for 2–3 minutes at the hotter temperature or until crisp and golden brown.
4. Tip the chips into a bowl with kitchen paper to remove oil. Return the pan to the heat and add the butter.
5. Fry the garlic and peppercorns for 1 minute then add the brandy and cream and bubble for 1 minute.
6. Transfer the steaks to two warm plates and stir any juices into the sauce.
7. Arrange the parsnips next to the steaks and spoon the sauce over the top.

SERVES: **4** | PREP TIME: **5 MINS** | COOKING TIME: **45 MINS**

Baked Potatoes with Crispy Prosciutto

4 medium baking potatoes
8 prosciutto slices
4 tbsp soured cream
2 tbsp chives, chopped

1. Preheat the oven to 220°C (200° fan), 430 F, gas 7.
2. Prick the potatoes with a fork and cook them in a microwave on high for
   5 minutes.
3. Wrap the potatoes in foil and bake in the oven for 40 minutes or until
   cooked through.
4. Meanwhile, dry-fry the prosciutto slices in batches until crisp – this should take
   1–2 minutes per batch.
5. Reserve 4 whole slices and crumble the rest into the soured cream.
6. When the potatoes are ready, carefully unwrap the foil and split in half.
7. Add a dollop of soured cream and a slice of crisp prosciutto to each one then
   sprinkle with chives.

SERVES: **2** | PREP TIME: **2 MINS** | COOKING TIME: **10-15 MINS**

Gammon with Pineapple and Chips

200 g / 7 oz / 2 cups / 1 ½ cup
  oven chips
2 tbsp olive oil
2 large gammon steaks
2 pineapple rings
150 g / 5 ½ oz / 1 cup frozen peas

1. Preheat the oven to 200°C (180° fan), 390 F, gas 6.
2. Spread the chips out on a baking tray and cook for 10 minutes or according to the packet instructions.
3. Meanwhile, heat the oil in a large frying pan and fry the gammon steaks for 3 minutes on each side.
4. While the gammon is cooking, boil the peas for 4 minutes then drain.
5. Move the gammon to the side of the frying pan and add the pineapple slices to heat through.
6. Serve the gammon with the pineapple on top and the chips and peas on the side.
7. Spoon over any of the juices that have come out of the gammon and pineapple.

SERVES: 4 | PREP TIME: **5 MINS** | COOKING TIME: **35 MINS**

Leek and Ham Gratin

6 leeks, trimmed and washed
2 tbsp olive oil
600 ml / 1 pint / 2 ½ cups whole milk
3 tbsp butter
1 tbsp plain (all purpose) flour
75 g / 2 ½ oz / ¾ cup Cheddar, grated
6 slices ham

1. Preheat the oven to 190°C (170° fan), 375 F, gas 5.
2. Rub the leeks with oil and bake them in the oven for 10 minutes.
3. Meanwhile, bring the milk to a simmer.
4. Heat the butter in a small saucepan then stir in the flour and cook for 1 minute.
5. Gradually incorporate the hot milk, stirring continuously to avoid any lumps forming.
6. Continue to stir until it starts to bubble then stir in the cheese and season with salt and pepper.
7. Take the leeks out of the oven and wrap each one with a piece of ham.
8. Return the leeks to the baking dish in a double layer and pour over the sauce, then season with plenty of black pepper.
9. Return the dish to the oven and cook for 20 minutes or until the leeks are soft and the sauce has browned at the edges.

Bacon, Egg and Cheese Bagels

12 rashers smoked streaky bacon
4 seeded bagels, halved horizontally
4 slices processed cheese
1 tbsp butter
6 large eggs, lightly beaten
salt and pepper

1. Cook the bacon in a hot frying pan for 3 minutes on each side.
2. Remove from the pan and keep warm, then add the bagel halves to the pan, cut side down and let them warm through.
3. Put the four bagel bases on plates and top with the cheese, followed by the bacon.
4. Melt the butter in a saucepan, then pour in the eggs. Stir over a medium heat until they scramble to your liking. Season to taste with salt and pepper, if desired.
5. Spoon the scrambled egg on top of the bacon, add the bagel lids and serve.

Sticky Sesame Chicken

8 chicken thighs
2 tbsp runny honey
2 tbsp soy sauce
½ orange, juiced
2 tbsp oyster sauce
½ tsp Chinese five spice powder
2 tsp sesame oil
2 tbsp sesame seeds
rice noodles and chives to serve

1. Preheat the oven to 200°C (180° fan), 390 F, gas 6.
2. Arrange the chicken thighs in a single layer in a snugly-fitting baking dish.
3. Mix the honey, soy, orange juice, oyster sauce, five spice and sesame oil together and pour it over the chicken.
4. Sprinkle with sesame seeds and bake for 35–40 minutes or until the chicken is cooked through.
5. If it starts to colour too quickly, cover the dish with foil.
6. Serve the chicken with rice noodles, garnished with chives.

Macaroni Cheese with Bacon

400 g / 14 oz / 4 cups dried macaroni
25 g / 1 oz butter
4 rashers streaky bacon, chopped
2 courgettes (zucchini), sliced
25 g / 1 oz / ¼ cup plain (all purpose)
  flour
600 ml / 1 pint / 2 ½ cups milk
150 g / 5 ½ oz / 1 ½ cups Cheddar
  cheese, grated

1. Preheat the oven to 180°C (160° fan), gas 4. Cook the macaroni in boiling, salted water according to the packet instructions or until al dente. Drain well.
2. Meanwhile, melt the butter in a medium saucepan then fry the bacon and courgettes for 2 minutes.
3. Remove the bacon and courgettes from the pan with a slotted spoon, then pour the flour into the pan.
4. Gradually whisk in the milk a little at a time until it is all incorporated. Cook the sauce over a low heat, stirring constantly, until the mixture thickens.
5. Take the pan off the heat and stir in the bacon and courgettes and half the cheese. Season to taste.
6. Stir the macaroni into the cheese sauce and scrape it into a baking dish.
7. Sprinkle over the remaining cheese then bake for 25 minutes or until the cheese is bubbling.

Chicken and Potato Gratin

450 g / 1 lb / 2 ½ cups Maris Piper
  potatoes, peeled and cubed
600 ml / 1 pint / 2 ½ cups whole milk
3 tbsp butter
1 tbsp plain (all purpose) flour
2 tbsp flat leaf parsley, chopped
450 g / 1 lb / 2 ¾ cups cooked chicken
15 g / ½ oz breadcrumbs

1. Boil the potatoes for 12 minutes, then drain well. Bring the milk to a simmer.
2. Mash the potatoes with 1 tablespoon of the butter and a little of the hot milk.
3. Heat 1 tablespoon of the butter in a saucepan and stir in the flour. Incorporate the rest of the hot milk. Stir until it bubbles then stir in the parsley and chicken.
4. Preheat the grill to its highest setting. Pour the chicken mixture into a baking dish and top with the mashed potato.
5. Dot the final tablespoon of butter over the top and sprinkle with breadcrumbs then grill for 5 minutes or until the top is golden and bubbling.

Cheese and Red Onion Burgers

2 beef burgers
1 red onion, peeled and sliced
2 tbsp olive oil
2 white baps
2 lettuce leaves
1 large tomato, sliced
4 slices mild Cheddar

1. Preheat the grill to its highest setting.
2. Put the burgers and onion slices on a grill tray and brush with olive oil. Grill for 4 minutes on each side or until the burgers are cooked to your liking and the onions are caramelised at the edges.
3. Cut the baps in half and add a lettuce leaf and the tomato slices to the bottom halves.
4. Top the tomato with the burgers and lay the cheese on top, followed by the onions.
5. Put the lids on the baps and serve.

SERVES: **4** | PREP TIME: **10 MINS** | COOKING TIME: **25 MINS**

Potatoes Stuffed with Bacon and Cheese

4 medium baking potatoes
150 g / 5 ½ oz / ⅔ cup streaky bacon, chopped
1 tbsp olive oil
2 tbsp crème fraiche
2 tbsp chives, chopped
4 slices Raclette cheese

1. Preheat the oven to 220°C (200° fan), 430 F, gas 7.
2. Prick the potatoes and cook them in a microwave on high for 5 minutes.
3. Meanwhile, fry the bacon in the oil for 4 minutes then stir in the crème fraiche and chives.
4. Cut a slice off the top of the potatoes and scoop out the centres with a teaspoon.
5. Mix 4 tablespoon of the scooped out potato with the bacon mixture, then stuff it back into the potato shells.
6. Lay a slice of Raclette over each potato then bake in the oven for 20 minutes or until golden brown.

SERVES: **6** | PREP TIME: **2 MINS** | COOKING TIME: **6 MINS**

Prosciutto and Quail Egg Crostini

6 slices baguette
½ clove garlic
2 tbsp olive oil
6 quail eggs
6 slices prosciutto

1. Preheat the grill to its highest setting.
2. Spread the baguette slices out on a grill tray and toast for 2 minutes on each side or until golden brown.
3. Rub the crostini with the halved garlic clove and brush with half of the olive oil.
4. Heat the rest of the oil in a large frying pan and break in the quail eggs. Fry the eggs for 2 minutes or until the whites are set.
5. Lay a slice of prosciutto on top of each crostini and top each one with a fried quail egg.

SERVES: **4** | PREP TIME: **20 MINS** | COOKING TIME: **10 MINS**

Steak Kebabs and Chips

400 g / 14 oz / 2 ⅓ cups oven chips
450 g / 1 lb / 2 cups sirloin steak, cubed
1 green pepper, cubed
1 onion, cubed
2 tbsp olive oil
1 lettuce, sliced
12 cherry tomatoes, halved
salt and pepper

1. Put 8 wooden skewers in a bowl of water and leave to soak for 20 minutes.
2. Preheat the oven to 200°C (180° fan), 390 F, gas 6.
3. Spread the chips out on a baking tray and cook for 10 minutes or according to the packet instructions.
4. Meanwhile, preheat a griddle pan until smoking hot.
5. Thread alternate chunks of steak, pepper and onion onto the skewers, brush with oil and season with salt and pepper.
6. Griddle the kebabs for 4 minutes on each side or until fully cooked through.
7. Sprinkle the chips with salt and pepper and divide between four warm plates. Serve 2 kebabs per person and arrange the lettuce and tomatoes on the side.

Pork and Brie Roulades

4 pork escallops
4 slices prosciutto
12 large basil leaves
8 slices Brie

1. Preheat the oven to 200°C (180° fan), 390 F, gas 6
2. Put the pork between 2 sheets of clingfilm and bash it flat with a rolling pin.
3. Peel off the cling film.
4. Lay the prosciutto slices out on a chopping board and top with the basil leaves.
5. Top each one with a piece of pork then lay the Brie on top.
6. Roll them up into roulades and secure with a skewer or cocktail stick.
7. Transfer the roulades to a roasting tin and cook in the oven for 25–30 minutes or until the pork is cooked in the centre.
8. Serve with spaghetti or a green salad.

Bacon and Onion Gratin

600 ml / 1 pint / 2 ½ cups whole milk
3 tbsp butter
1 tbsp plain (all-purpose) flour
75 g / 2 ½ oz / ¾ cup Cheddar, grated
8 rashers of smoked bacon
1 large onion, halved and thinly sliced

1. Preheat the oven to 190°C (170° fan), 375 F, gas 5 and bring the milk to a simmer.
2. Heat the butter in a small saucepan then stir in the flour and cook for 1 minute.
3. Gradually incorporate the hot milk, stirring continuously to avoid any lumps forming.
4. Continue to stir until it starts to bubble then stir in the cheese and season with salt and pepper.
5. Arrange the bacon and onions in four gratin dishes then spoon over the sauce.
6. Cook the gratins in the oven for 20 minutes or until the onions are cooked.

Chilli Con Carne

2 tbsp olive oil
2 shallots, finely chopped
1 red chilli (chili), finely chopped
2 cloves of garlic, crushed
½ tsp cayenne pepper
450 g / 1 lb / 2 cups minced beef
400 g / 14 oz / 2 cups canned tomatoes,
  chopped
200 ml / 7 fl. oz / 1 cup beef stock
400 g / 14 oz / 2 cups canned kidney
  beans, drained
a few sprigs coriander (cilantro) and
  boiled rice to serve

1. Heat the oil in a large saucepan and fry the shallot and chilli for 3 minutes,
   stirring occasionally.
2. Add the garlic and cayenne and cook for 2 minutes, then add the mince.
3. Fry the mince until it starts to brown then add the chopped tomatoes, stock
   and kidney beans and bring to a gentle simmer.
4. Cook the chilli con carne for 30 minutes, stirring occasionally, until the mince
   is tender and the sauce has thickened a little.
5. Taste for seasoning and add salt and freshly ground black pepper as necessary.
6. Serve with boiled rice and garnish with coriander.

Chicken with Vine Tomatoes

4 chicken breasts
4 small cherry tomato vines
3 tbsp olive oil
salt and pepper

1. Preheat the oven to 200°C (180° fan), 390 F, gas 6.
2. Rub the chicken and tomatoes with oil and arrange in a baking dish.
   Season well with salt and pepper.
3. Bake for 30 minutes or until the chicken is thoroughly cooked through and
   the tomatoes have softened and wrinkled.

SERVES: **4** | PREP TIME: **5 MINS** | COOKING TIME: **40 MINS**

Chicken and Red Onion Hot Pot

400 g / 14 oz Maris Piper potatoes,
  peeled and sliced
4 tbsp olive oil
1 red onion, sliced
200 g / 7 oz / 1 ¼ cups chicken
  breast, sliced
2 tsp Dijon mustard
300 ml / 10 ½ fl. oz / 1 ¼ cups
  white wine
50 g / 1 ¾ oz / ¼ cup butter, melted
salt and pepper

1. Preheat the oven to 220°C (200° fan), 430 F, gas 7 and put a baking dish in to heat.
2. Cook the potatoes in boiling salted water for 10 minutes or until tender. Drain well.
3. Meanwhile, heat the oil in a frying pan and cook the onions with a pinch of salt for 5 minutes.
4. Add the chicken and stir-fry for 3 minutes then stir in the mustard, pour in the wine, and bring to a simmer.
5. Spoon the chicken mixture into the preheated baking dish and arrange the potatoes on top.
6. Brush the potatoes with melted butter and sprinkle with salt and pepper, then bake for 30 minutes or until the potatoes are golden.

Green Pepper and Bacon Crustless Quiche

1 green pepper, very thinly sliced
2 rashers streaky bacon,
 very thinly sliced
2 tbsp olive oil
6 eggs
1 tbsp basil, finely shredded

1. Preheat the oven to 180°C (160° fan), 355 F, gas 4.
2. Fry the peppers and bacon in the oil for 10 minutes or until softened.
3. Lightly beat the eggs and stir in the peppers and bacon.
4. Pour the mixture into a non-stick cake tin and bake in the oven for 20–25 minutes or until just set in the centre.
5. Sprinkle with basil and serve warm or at room temperature.

Coddled Eggs with Bacon and Shallots

2 rashers smoked streaky bacon,
 thinly sliced
1 shallot, halved and thinly sliced
1 tbsp olive oil
1 tbsp tarragon, chopped
150g / 5 ½ oz / ⅔ cup crème fraiche
4 large eggs

1. Preheat the oven to 180°C (160° fan), 355 F, gas 4.
2. Fry the bacon and shallot in the oil for 2 minutes then stir in the tarragon and crème fraiche.
3. Divide half the mixture between four ramekin dishes and crack an egg into each one, then top with the rest of the crème fraiche mixture.
4. Put the ramekins in a roasting tin and add enough boiling water to the tin to come half way up the side of the ramekins.
5. Bake for 15 minutes or until the eggs are cooked to your liking, then serve immediately.

Chicken Salad Wraps

1 cooked chicken breast, diced
1 red pepper, diced
2 tomatoes, diced
¼ cucumber, diced
1 tbsp capers
50 g / 1 ¾ oz / 1 cup lamb's lettuce
4 tbsp mayonnaise
4 flour tortillas

1. Mix the chicken with the vegetables, capers and half of the lamb's lettuce and stir in the mayonnaise.
2. Divide the mixture between the tortillas and roll them up.
3. Cut each wrap in half and secure with cocktail sticks.
4. Serve with the rest of the lamb's lettuce on the side.

Poached Egg and Bacon Rolls

4 thick rashers streaky bacon
2 very fresh eggs
2 sesame rolls
2 lettuce leaves
1 large tomato, sliced

1. Preheat the grill to its highest setting and bring a wide saucepan of water to a gentle simmer.
2. Grill the bacon for 2 minutes on each side or until crisp and golden brown.
3. Meanwhile, crack each egg into a cup and pour them smoothly into the water, one at a time.
4. Simmer gently for 3 minutes.
5. Cut the rolls in half and add a lettuce leaf and a thick slice of tomato to the bottom halves.
6. Top the tomato with the bacon. Use a slotted spoon to take the eggs out of the water and blot the underneath on a piece of kitchen paper before laying them on top of the bacon.
7. Put the lids on the rolls and hold everything together with a wooden skewer.
8. Serve with roasted new potatoes and extra salad.

SERVES: 4 | PREP TIME: 30 MINS | COOKING TIME: 15 MINS

Pork and Turnip Kebabs

250 g / 9 oz / 1 ½ cup baby turnips
450 g / 1 lb / 3 cups pork belly,
  cut into cubes
3 tbsp soy sauce
1 tbsp runny honey
1 tsp sesame oil
2 tbsp sesame seeds
2 tbsp poppy seeds

1. Put 12 wooden skewers in a bowl of cold water and leave to soak for 20 minutes.
2. Meanwhile, cook the turnips in boiling salted water for 10 minutes or until tender. Drain well.
3. While the turnips are cooking, mix the soy sauce, honey and sesame oil together and use ¾ of the mixture to marinade the pork for 15 minutes.
4. Preheat the grill to its highest setting.
5. Thread the cooked turnips onto 4 of the skewers and brush them with the remaining marinade.
6. Thread the pork onto the final 8 skewers. Sprinkle 4 of the pork skewers with sesame seeds and the other 4 with poppy seeds.
7. Grill the kebabs for 4 minutes on each side or until the pork is cooked through.

SERVES: **4** | PREP TIME: **5 MINS** | COOKING TIME: **40 MINS**

Jacket Potatoes with Chilli Con Carne

2 tbsp olive oil
1 red onion, chopped
1 red pepper, chopped
2 cloves garlic, crushed
½ tsp cayenne pepper
450 g / 1 lb / 2 cups minced beef
400 g / 14 oz / 2 cups canned tomatoes, chopped
200 ml / 7 fl. oz / ¾ cup beef stock
400 g / 14 oz / 4 cups canned kidney beans, drained
4 baking potatoes
1 tbsp coriander (cilantro) leaves, chopped

1. Preheat the oven to 220°C (200° fan), 430 F, gas 7.
2. Heat the oil in a large saucepan and fry the onion and pepper for 3 minutes.
   Add the garlic and Cayenne and cook for 2 minutes, then add the mince.
3. Fry the mince until it starts to brown then add the chopped tomatoes,
   stock and kidney beans.
4. Cook the chilli con carne for 30 minutes, stirring occasionally, until the mince
   is tender and the sauce has thickened a little.
5. Meanwhile, prick the potatoes and microwave for 5 minutes. Transfer to the
   oven a bake for 25 minutes.
6. Taste the chilli for seasoning and add salt and freshly ground black pepper
   as necessary.
7. Cut the potatoes in half and spoon over the chilli then sprinkle with coriander.

SERVES: **4** | PREP TIME: **5 MINS** | COOKING TIME: **40 MINS**

Baked Potatoes Stuffed with Sausage Meat

4 medium baking potatoes
8 good quality pork sausages, skinned
1 tbsp wholegrain mustard
1 clove garlic, crushed

1. Preheat the oven to 220°C (200° fan), 430 F, gas 7.
2. Prick the potatoes and cook them in a microwave on high for 5 minutes.
3. Cut a slice off the top of the potatoes and scoop out the centres into a bowl.
4. Mix it with the sausage meat, mustard and garlic, then stuff it back into the potato shells.
5. Turn the sliced-off sections cut side up and put them on top of the stuffing.
6. Bake in the oven for 35 minutes or until golden brown and cooked through.

Savoury Pancakes with Ham and Mushroom

50 g / 1 ¾ oz / ¼ cup butter
200 g / 7 oz / 2 cups / 2 ⅔ cups button mushrooms, chopped
1 tbsp plain (all-purpose) flour
300 ml / 10 ½ fl. oz / 1 ⅕ cups milk
100 g / 3 ½ oz / ⅔ cup ham, chopped
8 ready-made pancakes

1. Preheat the oven to 200°C (180° fan), 390 F, gas 6.
2. Melt the butter in a large saucepan and fry the mushrooms with a pinch of salt for 5 minutes.
3. Stir in the flour then gradually incorporate the milk, stirring continuously to avoid any lumps forming.
4. When the mixture starts to bubble, stir in the ham and a grind of black pepper then take the pan off the heat.
5. Lay the pancakes out on the work surface and divide the mushroom mixture between them.
6. Roll the pancakes up and transfer them to a baking tray then bake for 10 minutes or until golden brown.

Fish Dishes

SERVES: **4** | PREP TIME: **10 MINS** | COOKING TIME: **2-4 MINS**

Battered Prawns

2–3 litres / 3 ½ pints–5 pints /
  8–12 cups sunflower oil

110 g / 4 oz / ½ cup plain (all-purpose)
  flour

2 large eggs

24 raw king prawns (shrimps), peeled
  with tails left intact

salt and pepper

1. Heat the oil in a deep fat fryer, according to the manufacturer's instructions, to a temperature of 180°C.
2. Mix the flour with a big pinch of salt and pepper.
3. Make a well in the centre and break in the eggs, then incorporate all the flour from around the outside with a whisk.
4. Hold the prawns by their tails and dip them into the batter then drop them straight into the hot oil.
5. Fry for 1–2 minutes, turning halfway through, until they are crisp and golden brown.
6. Transfer the prawns to a kitchen paper lined bowl to absorb the excess oil then serve immediately.

SERVES: **4** | PREP TIME: **15 MINS** | COOKING TIME: **3-4 MINS**

Deep Fried Fish Balls

400 g / 14 oz / 2 cups white fish fillets
4 spring onions (scallions), chopped
1 clove garlic, crushed
50 g / 1 ¾ oz / ⅓ cup black olives, pitted
1 tsp ground cumin
½ tsp ground coriander (cilantro)
½ tsp ground cinnamon
2–3 litres / 3 ½ pints–5 pints / 8–12 cups sunflower oil
lettuce leaves, to serve

1. Put the fish, spring onions, garlic, olives and spices in a food processor with a big pinch of salt and whizz to a sticky paste.
2. Heat the oil in a deep fat fryer, according to the manufacturer's instructions, to a temperature of 180°C.
3. Use an ice cream scoop to portion the mixture into balls and drop them straight into the hot oil.
4. Fry the fish balls for 3–4 minutes, turning once, or until they are golden brown.
5. Line a large bowl with a thick layer of kitchen paper and when they are ready, tip them into the bowl to remove any excess oil.
6. Sprinkle with a little sea salt to taste and serve immediately on a bed of lettuce.

SERVES: 3 | PREP TIME: 20 MINS | COOKING TIME: 8 MINS

Bacon-wrapped Scallop Kebabs

12 scallops
6 thin slices streaky bacon, halved
12 button mushrooms
1 lime, cut into wedges
fresh coriander (cilantro) leaves
   to garnish

1. Put 6 wooden skewers in a bowl of water and leave to soak for 20 minutes.
2. Preheat the grill to its highest setting.
3. Wrap the scallops in bacon then thread them onto the skewers with the mushrooms.
4. Grill the kebabs for 4 minutes on each side or until they are golden brown and garnish with lime and coriander.

SERVES: 4 | PREP TIME: 5 MINS | COOKING TIME: 2 MINS

Gravadlax and Caper Bagels

2 bagels, halved horizontally
2 tbsp cream cheese
12 thick slices gravadlax
1 tbsp baby capers
4 sprigs dill

1. Lightly toast the bagel halves for 2 minutes and spread them with a generous layer of cream cheese.
2. Season to taste with black pepper.
3. Top each bagel with three slices of gravadlax, a few baby capers and a sprig of dill.
4. Serve immediately.

SERVES: **2** | PREP TIME: **5 MINS** | COOKING TIME: **5-8 MINS**

Butterflied Bream with Grilled Tomatoes

2 small sea bream, scaled, filleted and butterflied
1 large tomato, sliced
2 tbsp olive oil
1 tsp runny honey
1 tbsp white wine vinegar
2 tbsp walnut oil
1 tbsp flat leaf parsley, finely chopped
2 tbsp kalamata olives
2 tbsp caperberries

1. Preheat the grill to its highest setting.
2. Arrange the bream, skin side up, on a large grill pan and surround with the tomato slices.
3. Brush the bream and tomatoes with olive oil and season well with salt and pepper, then grill for 3 minutes.
4. Turn the fish and tomatoes over and grill for 2 more minutes.
5. Meanwhile, whisk the honey and vinegar into the walnut oil and stir in the parsley.
6. When the fish is ready, transfer it to two warm plates and garnish with the grilled tomato slices, olives and capers.
7. Drizzle over the dressing and serve immediately.

SERVES: 4 | **PREP TIME: 10 MINS** | **COOKING TIME: 5 MINS**

Red Mullet Crostini with Tomato Salsa

2 tbsp olive oil
8 red mullet fillets
4 slices baguette
mixed salad leaves to serve

FOR THE SALSA
2 tomatoes
1 shallot, finely chopped
1 tbsp chives, finely chopped
1 tbsp flat leaf parsley, finely chopped
1 tbsp white wine vinegar
3 tbsp extra virgin olive oil

1. Score a cross in the top of the tomatoes and blanch them in boiling water for 30 seconds.
2. Plunge them into cold water then peel off the skins.
3. Cut the tomatoes in half and remove the seeds, then cut the flesh into small cubes.
4. Stir the shallot and herbs into the tomato then whisk in the vinegar and oil. Season to taste with salt and pepper.
5. Heat the oil in an ovenproof frying pan. Season the red mullet fillets with salt and pepper and fry, skin side down, for 2 minutes.
6. Turn the fillets over then turn off the heat and leave them to cook in the heat of the pan for 1 minute.
7. While the fish is cooking, toast the bread.
8. Arrange the mullet on top of the crostini and drizzle over the vinaigrette. Garnish with mixed salad leaves.

SERVES: **2** | PREP TIME: **4 MINS** | COOKING TIME: **8-10 MINS**

Griddled Salmon with Summer Vegetables

75 g / 2 ½ oz / ½ cup French beans
75 g / 2 ½ oz / ½ cup fresh peas
1 courgette (zucchini)
2 portions salmon fillet, skinned
3 tbsp olive oil
75 g / 2 ½ oz / ¾ cup mange tout
1 tbsp garden mint, chopped
1 tbsp flat leaf parsley, chopped
½ lemon, juiced

1. Blanch the French beans and peas for 4 minutes then drain and refresh in cold water.
2. Use a vegetable peeler to shave the courgette into long ribbons.
3. Heat a griddle pan until smoking hot on the stove.
4. Brush the salmon fillets with 1 tablespoon of the oil and season with salt and pepper.
5. Griddle the salmon for 2 minutes on each side.
6. Meanwhile, heat the rest of the oil in a large sauté pan and add the beans, peas, courgette ribbons and mange tout.
7. Stir-fry the vegetables for 4 minutes then sprinkle over the herbs and a squeeze of lemon juice.
8. Spoon the vegetables into a warm serving dish. Turn the salmon fillets in any lemony juices left in the sauté pan before arranging them on top of the vegetables.

SERVES: **2** | PREP TIME: **10 MINS** | COOKING TIME: **1 MIN**

Marinated Anchovies with Tomato Salsa

2 medium tomatoes
1 tbsp fresh basil leaves, chopped
1 tbsp flat leaf parsley, chopped
1 tsp fresh young rosemary, finely chopped
4 tbsp extra virgin olive oil
16 marinated anchovy fillets

1. Score a cross in the top of the tomatoes and blanch in boiling water for 30 seconds. When the skin of the tomatoes starts to curl up, remove them with a slotted spoon and dunk in a bowl of cold water.

2. Peel off and discard the skins then cut them in half and remove the seeds. Chop the tomato flesh into small cubes.

3. Mix the herbs with the olive oil, a pinch of salt and plenty of freshly ground black pepper.

4. Arrange the anchovy fillets on 2 plates and spoon some of the herb oil on top.

5. Stir the rest of the herb oil into the chopped tomatoes and divide between the two plates.

Grilled Salmon with Honey and Lime

2 tbsp runny honey
2 tbsp light soy sauce
2 limes, sliced
4 portions salmon fillet, skinned

1. Mix the honey with the soy and stir in the limes then pour it over the salmon. Leave to marinate for 25 minutes.
2. Preheat the grill to its highest setting.
3. Arrange the salmon and lime slices on a large grill tray and grill for 3 minutes on each side or until the glaze is golden and sticky and the salmon is just cooked in the centre.

Seared Salmon with Vegetable Broth

1 litre / 1 pint 15 fl. oz / 4 cups good quality fish stock
2 tsp yellow miso paste
1 courgette (zucchini), cubed
2 tomatoes, peeled and cubed
4 spring onions, chopped
2 tbsp olive oil
8 slices salmon fillet

TO SERVE
2 tbsp candied orange peel, finely chopped
2 tbsp chives, finely chopped
1 tbsp light soy sauce
1 tsp sesame oil

1. Bring the fish stock to a simmer and stir in the yellow miso paste and courgette. Simmer for 4 minutes then add the tomatoes and spring onion and simmer for another 2 minutes.
2. Meanwhile, heat the olive oil in a large frying pan until smoking hot and season the salmon at the last minute with salt and pepper.
3. Sear the salmon slices for 1 minute on each side or until golden brown.
4. Put the vegetable broth in 4 bowls and top each one with 2 slices of salmon.
5. Mix the candied peel with the chives, soy sauce and sesame oil and spoon it over the salmon.

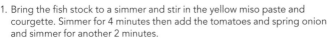

King Prawn and Fennel Salad

1 fennel bulb, finely chopped
1 tbsp fennel tops, chopped plus extra
  for garnishing
3 tbsp mayonnaise
1 tbsp lemon juice
12 cooked king prawns (shrimps),
  peeled leaving tails intact
a small bunch chives

1. Mix the fennel and fennel tops with the mayonnaise and lemon juice and season well with salt and pepper.
2. Use a ring mould or pastry cutter to shape the salad onto the plates and top each one with 3 prawns.
3. Garnish with chives and fennel tops.

Prawn Stir-fry with Vegetables

3 tbsp olive oil
1 red chilli (chili), finely chopped
1 clove of garlic, crushed
20 raw king prawns (shrimp), peeled
  leaving tails intact
200 g / 7 oz / 2 cups mangetout,
  trimmed
100 g / 3 ½ oz / ¾ cup canned straw
  mushrooms, drained
2 tbsp soy sauce
100 g / 3 ½ oz / 1 cup bean sprouts

1. Heat the oil in a large wok and fry the chilli and garlic for 30 seconds.
2. Add the prawns, mange tout and mushrooms and stir-fry for 3 minutes or until the prawns turn opaque.
3. Add the soy and bean sprouts and cook for 1 more minute then serve immediately.

Clam Omelette

3 large eggs
10 g / 1 tbsp butter
50 g / 1 ¾ oz / ¼ cup cooked shelled clams
1 tbsp flat leaf parsley, finely chopped

1. Break the eggs into a jug with a pinch of salt and pepper and beat them gently to break up the yolks.
2. Heat the butter in a non-stick frying pan until sizzling then pour in the eggs.
3. Cook over a medium heat until the eggs start to set around the outside. Use a spatula to draw the sides of the omelette into the centre and tilt the pan to fill the gaps with more liquid egg.
4. Repeat the process until the top of the omelette is just set, then sprinkle over the clams and parsley.
5. Shake the omelette out onto a plate, folding it over as you go.

Garlic Salmon with Sesame Seeds

1 egg white, beaten
1 tbsp cornflour
2 portions salmon fillet, skinned
50 g / 1 ¾ oz / ¼ cup sesame seeds
4 tbsp olive oil
1 clove garlic, crushed
2 tbsp soy sauce

1. Mix the egg white with the cornflour and brush a thin layer onto one side of the salmon. Dip the salmon in the sesame seeds, pressing down firmly to ensure they stick.
2. Heat half the oil in a large frying pan and cook the salmon, sesame side down, for 4 minutes.
3. Meanwhile, heat the rest of the oil in a sauté pan and fry the garlic for 2 minutes. Stir in the soy sauce and 1 tablespoon of water.
4. Turn the salmon over, turn off the heat and let the other side cook in the residual heat of the pan for 2 minutes.
5. Arrange the salmon fillets on two warm dinner plates and pour over the fried garlic in soy sauce, allowing it to soak into the salmon.
6. Serve with rosemary and vegetables.

SERVES: **2** | PREP TIME: **20 MINS** | COOKING TIME: **8 MINS**

Sardine and Cherry Tomato Skewers

8 sardines
8 cherry tomatoes
2 tbsp olive oil

1. Put 8 wooden skewers in a bowl of water and leave to soak for 20 minutes.
2. Preheat the grill to its highest setting.
3. Cut the heads off the sardines and thread them onto the skewers with the tomatoes.
4. Brush them with oil and sprinkle with a little salt and pepper then grill for 4 minutes on each side or until cooked through.

SERVES: **4** | PREP TIME: **10 MINS** | COOKING TIME: **20 MINS**

Tuna and Courgette Tortilla

4 tbsp olive oil

1 courgette (zucchini), quartered and sliced

6 free-range eggs

200 g / 7 oz / 1 cup canned tuna, drained and flaked

oregano to garnish

1. Heat half the oil in a non-stick frying pan and fry the courgettes for 5 minutes.
2. Meanwhile, gently beat the eggs in a jug to break up the yolks. When the courgettes are ready, stir them into the eggs with the tuna and season with a little salt and pepper.
3. Heat the rest of the oil in the frying pan then pour in the egg mixture.
4. Cook over a gentle heat for 6–8 minutes or until the egg has set around the outside, but the centre is still a bit runny.
5. Turn it out onto a plate, then slide it back into the pan and cook the other side for 4–6 minutes.
6. Leave to cool for 5 minutes then cut into large wedges and serve, garnished with oregano.

Spicy Crab Pancakes

125 g / 4 ½ oz / ¾ cup plain
(all purpose) flour
1 tsp baking powder
1 large egg
150 ml / 5 ½ fl. oz / ⅔ cup milk
15 g / ½ oz butter, melted

1 red chilli (chili), finely chopped
1 clove of garlic, crushed
1 tsp root ginger, grated
100 g / 3 ½ oz / ½ cup fresh crab meat
2 spring onions (scallions), thinly sliced

1. Mix the flour and baking powder in a bowl and make a well in the centre.
   Break in the egg and pour in the milk then use a whisk to gradually
   incorporate all of the flour from around the outside.
2. Melt the butter in a small frying pan then whisk it into the batter.
3. Stir in the chilli, garlic, ginger and crab meat.
4. Put the buttered frying pan back over a low heat. Add a quarter of the
   pancake batter to the pan and cook for 2 minutes or until small bubbles
   start to appear on the surface.
5. Turn the pancake over with a spatula and cook the other side until golden
   brown and cooked through.
6. Repeat with the rest of the mixture to make another 3 large pancakes.
7. Serve the pancakes sprinkled with spring onion.

Vegetable Dishes

SERVES: 4 | PREP TIME: 20 MINS | COOKING TIME: 8 MINS

Courgettes Stuffed with Goats' Cheese

4 courgettes (zucchini)
150 g / 5 ½ oz / 1 cup fresh goats'
  cheese
1 tsp lemon zest, finely grated
2 tbsp chives, chopped

TO SERVE
4 large tomatoes, diced
2 tbsp olive oil
½ lemon, juiced
basil leaves, to garnish

1. Cut the ends off the courgettes and remove the middles with an apple corer.
2. Mix the goats' cheese with the lemon zest and chives and plenty of black pepper, then pack it into the cavities.
3. Steam the courgettes for 8 minutes or until tender, then slice and serve on a bed of tomatoes.
4. Drizzle over the oil and lemon and garnish with basil.

SERVES: **4** | PREP TIME: **15 MINS** | COOKING TIME: **5 MINS**

Kidney Bean Pâté

2 tbsp olive oil
1 red onion, finely chopped
2 cloves of garlic, crushed
½ tsp ground cumin
½ tsp ground coriander (cilantro)
400 g / 14 oz / 2 cups canned kidney beans, drained
2 tbsp soured cream
1 spring onion (scallion), chopped
tortilla chips to serve

1. Heat the oil in a frying pan and fry the onion and garlic for 5 minutes, stirring occasionally.
2. Scrape it into a food processor and add the spices, kidney beans and soured cream then season with salt and pepper.
3. Pulse the machine until the ingredients are finely chopped and well mixed, then spoon the pâté into a serving bowl and sprinkle with spring onion.
4. Serve with tortilla chips for dipping.

Lemon and Asparagus Risotto

1 litre / 1 pint 15 fl. oz / 4 cups good
quality vegetable stock
2 tbsp olive oil
1 onion, finely chopped
2 cloves of garlic, crushed
1 lemon, zest finely pared
150 g / 5 ½ oz / ¾ cup risotto rice
100 g / 3 ½ oz / 1 cup asparagus
spears, cut into short lengths
2 tbsp butter

1. Heat the stock in a saucepan.
2. Heat the olive oil in a sauté pan
   and gently fry the onion for
   5 minutes without colouring.
3. Add the garlic and lemon zest and
   cook for 2 more minutes then stir
   in the rice.
4. When it is well coated with the oil,
   add the asparagus, followed by
   2 ladles of the hot stock.
5. Cook, stirring occasionally, until
   most of the stock has been
   absorbed before adding the
   next 2 ladles.
6. Continue in this way for around
   15 minutes or until the rice is
   just tender.
7. Stir in the butter, then cover the
   pan and take off the heat to rest
   for 4 minutes.
8. Uncover the pan and season well
   with salt and pepper, then spoon
   into warm bowls.

Leek, Tomato and Cheese Quiche

2 leeks, sliced
2 tbsp butter
3 large eggs, beaten
225 ml / 8 fl. oz / 1 cup double cream
100 g / 3 ½ oz / ¾ cup cherry tomatoes,
    quartered
150 g / 5 ½ oz / 1 ½ cups Gruyère, grated
1 ready-made pastry case

1. Preheat the oven to 150°C (130° fan), 300 F, gas 2.
2. Fry the leeks in the butter with a pinch of salt for 5 minutes or until starting
   to soften.
3. Whisk the eggs with the double cream until smoothly combined then stir in
   the leeks, tomatoes and half of the Gruyère. Season generously with salt
   and pepper.
4. Pour the filling into the pastry case and scatter the rest of the cheese on top.
5. Bake for 35 minutes or until just set in the centre.

Mushroom and Spring Greens Stir-fry

3 tbsp vegetable oil
2 cloves garlic, finely chopped
1 tbsp root ginger, finely chopped
200 g / 7 oz / 2 cups / 2 ⅔ cup
    mushrooms, sliced
1 spring green cabbage, shredded
6 spring onions (scallions),
    sliced diagonally
2 tbsp rice wine or dry sherry
1 tsp caster (superfine) sugar
1 tbsp light soy sauce

1. Heat the oil in a large wok and fry the garlic, ginger and onion for 30 seconds.
2. Add the mushrooms and cabbage and stir-fry for 4 minutes then add the
   spring onions and stir-fry for 2 minutes.
3. Mix the rice wine, sugar and soy together and add it to the wok.
4. Stir-fry for 1 more minute then serve immediately.

SERVES: 4 | PREP TIME: 5 MINS | COOKING TIME: 8 MINS

Stir-fried Tofu with Vegetables

2 tbsp vegetable oil
2 cloves garlic, finely chopped
1 tbsp root ginger, finely chopped
200 g / 7 oz / 1 ¼ cups firm tofu, cubed
75 g / 2 ½ oz / ¾ cup baby sweetcorn, halved lengthways
75 g / 2 ½ oz / ¾ cup mange tout
½ tsp cornflour
2 tbsp rice wine or dry sherry
1 tsp caster (superfine) sugar
1 tbsp light soy sauce
75 g / 2 ½ oz / 1 ½ cups alfalfa sprouts
boiled rice to serve

1. Heat the oil in a large wok and fry the garlic and ginger for 30 seconds.
2. Add the tofu and stir-fry for 2 minutes then add the baby corn
   and mange tout and stir-fry for another 2 minutes.
3. Mix the cornflour with the rice wine, sugar and soy and add it to the wok.
4. Stir-fry for 2 more minutes then serve immediately, garnished
   with the alfalfa sprouts on a bed of rice.

SERVES: 4 | PREP TIME: 5 MINS | COOKING TIME: 12 MINS

Omelette with Broccoli and Noodles

200 g / 7 oz / 2 cups thin egg noodles
½ head broccoli, broken into florets
2 tbsp vegetable oil
2 cloves of garlic, thinly sliced
1 tbsp root ginger, thinly sliced
3 large eggs, beaten
2 tbsp light soy sauce

1. Cook the noodles in boiling salted water according to the packet instructions or until al dente, then drain well.
2. Meanwhile, blanch the broccoli for 4 minutes then plunge into cold water and drain well.
3. Heat the oil in a large wok and fry the garlic and ginger for 1 minute.
4. Pour the eggs into the pan and shake it while it sets into a thin omelette.
5. Use a fish slice to remove the omelette from the pan and cut it into squares.
6. Put the wok back on the heat and add the omelette, soy sauce, noodles and broccoli and stir-fry for 2 more minutes.

SERVES: 4 | PREP TIME: 10 MINS | COOKING TIME: 20 MINS

Mixed Vegetable Tortilla

4 tbsp olive oil

1 red onion, thinly sliced

1 red pepper, finely chopped

3 boiled potatoes, cooled and cubed

75 g / 2 ½ oz / ½ cup frozen peas, defrosted

6 eggs

1. Heat half the oil in a non-stick frying pan and fry the onion and peppers for 5 minutes.
2. Meanwhile, gently beat the eggs in a jug to break up the yolks. When the onions are ready, stir them into the eggs with the potatoes and peas and season with salt and pepper.
3. Heat the rest of the oil in the frying pan then pour in the egg mixture.
4. Cook over a gentle heat for 6 – 8 minutes or until the egg has set round the outside, but the centre is still a bit runny.
5. Turn it out onto a plate, then slide it back into the pan and cook the other side for 4 – 6 minutes.
6. Leave to cool for 5 minutes then cut into wedges and serve.

Spring Vegetables with Herb Cream

100 g / 3 ½ oz / 1 cup asparagus spears
6 baby celery hearts
100 g / 3 ½ oz / 1 cup green beans
100 g / 3 ½ oz / ⅔ cup baby carrots
100 g / 3 ½ oz / 1 cup fresh peas
300 ml / 10 ½ fl. oz / 1 ½ cup
  double cream
1 tbsp lemon juice
2 tbsp dill, chopped
2 tbsp coriander (cilantro) leaves,
  chopped
2 tbsp flat leaf parsley, chopped

1. Steam the vegetables for 6 minutes or until tender.
2. Meanwhile, heat the cream in a small saucepan until almost at a simmer then take off the heat and stir in the lemon juice and herbs. Season to taste with salt and white pepper.
3. Arrange the vegetables on four warm plates and spoon over the cream.

Halloumi and Parsley Omelette

3 large eggs
2 tbsp flat leaf parsley
50 g / 1 ¾ oz / ½ cup Halloumi, cubed
1 tbsp butter
½ tsp pink peppercorns, crushed

1. Break the eggs into a jug with a pinch of salt and pepper and beat them gently to break up the yolks.
2. Stir in the parsley and Halloumi.
3. Heat the butter in a non-stick frying pan until sizzling then pour in the eggs.
4. Cook over a medium heat until the eggs start to set around the outside. Use a spatula to draw the sides of the omelette into the centre and tilt the pan to fill the gaps with more liquid egg.
5. Repeat the process until the top of the omelette is just set then sprinkle over the pink peppercorns.

SERVES: 4 | PREP TIME: **10 MINS** | COOKING TIME: **30 MINS**

Potatoes with Mushrooms and Feta

4 medium baking potatoes
25 g / 1 oz butter
200 g / 7 oz / 2 cups / 2 ⅔ cup button mushrooms, sliced
2 cloves garlic, chopped
100 g / 3 ½ oz / ⅔ cup feta, crumbled

TO SERVE
2 tbsp pesto
a few sprigs parsley

1. Preheat the oven to 220°C (200° fan), 430 F, gas 7.
2. Prick the potatoes and cook them in a microwave on high for 8 minutes.
3. Cut them in half and scoop out the centres and arrange, cut side up, in a roasting tin.
4. Bake the potatoes for 20 minutes or until cooked through.
5. Meanwhile, melt the butter in a frying pan and fry the mushrooms with a pinch of salt for 10 minutes or until any juices that come out have evaporated and they start to colour.
6. Crumble in the feta and season well with freshly ground black pepper.
7. When the potatoes are ready, spoon the mushroom and feta mixture into the cavities and serve 2 halves per person with a drizzle of pesto and a sprig of parsley.

SERVES: **2** | PREP TIME: **10 MINS** | COOKING TIME: **4 MINS**

Goats' Cheese and Courgette Ciabatta

1 courgette (zucchini), sliced
   lengthways
2 tbsp olive oil
1 ciabatta roll, halved
4 tomatoes, halved
60 g / 2 oz / ⅓ cup fresh goats' cheese
½ tsp pink peppercorns, crushed
2 sprigs flat leaf parsley

1. Preheat a griddle pan until smoking hot.
2. Brush the courgette slices with half of the oil and season with salt and pepper.
3. Griddle the courgettes for 2 minutes on each side or until nicely marked.
4. Toast the ciabatta halves then brush them with the rest of the oil.
5. Arrange the courgette slices on top with the tomatoes and goats' cheese, then sprinkle with pink peppercorns and garnish with parsley.

Tofu and Spring Onion Omelette

3 large eggs
50 g / 1 ¾ oz / ¼ cup firm tofu, cubed
2 spring onions (scallions), chopped
flat leaf parsley to garnish
1 tbsp butter
2 tbsp flat leaf parsley

1. Break the eggs into a jug with a pinch of salt and pepper and beat them gently to break up the yolks.
2. Stir in the tofu and spring onions.
3. Heat the butter in a non-stick frying pan until sizzling then pour in the eggs.
4. Cook over a medium heat until the eggs start to set around the outside. Use a spatula to draw the sides of the omelette into the centre and tilt the pan to fill the gaps with more liquid egg.
5. Repeat the process until the top of the omelette is just set then fold in half and sprinkle over the parsley.

Roasted Mushrooms with Garlic

4 large mushrooms
2 tbsp olive oil
25 g / 1 oz butter
4 cloves garlic, chopped
2 tbsp flat leaf parsley, chopped

1. Preheat the oven to 200°C (180° fan), 390 F, gas 6.
2. Remove the stalks from the mushrooms and arrange cut side up in a baking dish.
3. Brush the mushrooms with oil and roast for 20 minutes.
4. Heat the butter in a small frying pan and cook the garlic until it just starts to turn golden, then quickly spoon the garlic butter over the mushrooms and sprinkle with parsley.

Penne with Broccoli and Garlic

1 bulb of garlic, cloves separated
400 g / 14 oz / 4 cups penne
1 small head broccoli, broken into florets
6 tbsp olive oil
30 g / 1 oz / ¼ cup Parmesan

1. Cook the garlic cloves in a large saucepan of boiling salted water for
   15 minutes.
2. Add the penne to the pan and cook according to the packet instructions
   or until al dente.
3. 4 minutes before the end of cooking time, add the broccoli to the pan.
4. Reserve 1 ladle of the cooking water and drain the rest then toss the
   penne, broccoli and garlic cloves with the oil and season with salt and pepper.
5. If the pasta looks a bit dry, add a little of the cooking water and shake the
   pan to emulsify.
6. Divide the pasta between four warm bowls and use a vegetable peeler to
   shave over some Parmesan.
7. The softened garlic can be squeezed out of the skins at the table and eaten
   with the pasta.

Courgette and Goats' Cheese Omelette

1 courgette (zucchini), coarsely grated
4 large eggs, beaten
50 g / 1 ¾ oz / ⅓ cup goats' cheese, crumbled
2 tbsp olive oil
flat leaf parsley, to garnish

1. Wrap the grated courgette in a clean tea towel and squeeze to get rid of any excess moisture.
2. Stir it into the eggs with the goats' cheese and season well with salt and pepper.
3. Heat half the oil in a frying pan and pour in half the egg mixture.
4. Shake the pan over a medium heat until the eggs set into a thin omelette.
5. Use a palette knife to transfer the omelette to a warm plate and cook the second one in the same way.
6. Garnish with flat leaf parsley and serve immediately.

Fusilli with Mixed Vegetables

400 g / 14 oz / 5 cups fusilli pasta
4 tbsp olive oil
4 cloves garlic, crushed
1 red pepper, cubed
½ head broccoli, broken into small florets
1 carrot, shredded
1 courgette (zucchini), shredded

1. Cook the fusilli in boiling salted water according to the packet instructions or until al dente.
2. While the pasta is cooking, heat the olive oil in a large frying pan and cook the garlic, peppers and broccoli for 5 minutes, stirring occasionally.
3. Add the shredded carrot and courgette to the pan and cook for 2 more minutes.
4. Reserve 1 ladle of the pasta cooking water and drain the rest then stir the pasta into the frying pan.
5. If it looks a bit dry, add some of the cooking water and shake the pan to emulsify.
6. Divide the pasta between four warm bowls and serve.

SERVES: **4** | PREP TIME: **1 MIN** | COOKING TIME: **12 MINS**

Butterbeans with Mushrooms

4 large portobello mushrooms
50 g / 1 ¾ oz / ¼ cup butter
200 g / 7 oz / 2 cups / 2 ⅔ cup wild
  mushrooms, cleaned
2 cloves garlic, crushed
100 ml / 3 ½ fl. oz / ½ cup
  double cream
100 g / 3 ½ oz / ⅔ cup canned
  butterbeans, drained
2 tbsp chives, chopped
extra whole chives to garnish

1. Preheat the oven to 200°C (180°
   fan), 390 F, gas 6.
2. Remove the stalks from the
   portobello mushrooms and arrange
   cut side up in a baking dish.
3. Add 1 teaspoon of the butter to
   the centre of each and roast for
   20 minutes.
4. Heat the rest of the butter in a
   frying pan and cook wild
   mushrooms for 6 minutes.
5. Add the garlic and continue to
   cook for 2 minutes, then add the
   cream and butterbeans and bring
   to a simmer.
6. Season to taste with salt and
   pepper then stir in the chives.
7. Put a portobello mushroom on
   each plate and spoon over the
   wild mushroom mixture.
8. Decorate each one with a few
   whole chives.

SERVES: **4** | PREP TIME: **10 MINS** | COOKING TIME: **20 MINS**

Tortilla Español

4 tbsp olive oil
1 onion, thinly sliced
6 eggs
4 boiled potatoes, cooled and cubed

1. Heat half the oil in a non-stick frying pan and fry the onion with a pinch of salt and pepper for 5 minutes.
2. Meanwhile, gently beat the eggs in a jug to break up the yolks. When the onions are ready, stir them into the eggs with the potatoes and season with salt and pepper.
3. Heat the rest of the oil in the frying pan then pour in the egg mixture.
4. Cook over a gentle heat for 6–8 minutes or until the egg has set around the outside, but the centre is still a bit runny.
5. Turn it out onto a plate, then slide it back into the pan and cook the other side for 4–6 minutes.
6. Leave to cool for 5 minutes then cut into wedges and serve.

Sautéed Potatoes with Cumin and Thyme

800 g / 1 lb 12 oz / 5 ⅓ cups
  Charlotte potatoes
4 tbsp olive oil
1 tsp ground cumin
2 tbsp fresh thyme leaves

1. Boil the potatoes in salted water for 8 minutes then drain well and leave to steam dry for 2 minutes.
2. Heat the oil in a large sauté pan.
3. Sprinkle the potatoes with cumin, thyme and plenty of salt and pepper then fry for 10 minutes, shaking the pan and stirring occasionally.

Spiced Tomato Flatbreads

½ tsp mustard seeds
½ tsp cumin seeds
½ tsp coriander (cilantro) seeds
½ tsp chilli flakes
3 tbsp olive oil
1 onion, thinly sliced
1 clove garlic, crushed
3 tomatoes, cut into wedges
2 tbsp coriander leaves, chopped
2 flatbreads
50 g / 1 ¾ oz / ½ cup Emmental, grated

1. Preheat the oven to 220°C (200° fan), 430 F, gas 7 and put a baking tray in to heat.
2. Grind the spices with a pestle and mortar to a rough powder.
3. Heat the oil in a frying pan and fry the onion and spices for 10 minutes or until starting to caramelize.
4. Add the garlic and tomatoes to the pan and cook for 2 minutes to heat through.
5. Stir in the coriander leaves then divide the mixture between the flatbreads and sprinkle over the cheese.
6. Bake for 8 minutes to toast the tops and warm through the bread.

SERVES: 2 | PREP TIME: 5 MINS | COOKING TIME: 15 MINS

Tomato, Mushroom and Pepper Risotto

500 ml / 17 ½ fl. oz / 2 cups
vegetable stock
500 ml / 17 ½ fl. oz / 2 ¼ cups canned
tomatoes, chopped
2 tbsp olive oil
1 onion, finely chopped
1 yellow pepper, sliced
2 cloves of garlic, crushed
100 g / 3 ½ oz / 1 cup mushrooms,
sliced
150 g / 5 ½ oz / ¾ cup risotto rice
2 tbsp butter
basil leaves to garnish

1. Heat the stock and chopped tomatoes together in a saucepan.
2. Heat the olive oil in a sauté pan and gently fry the onion and peppers for 5 minutes without colouring.
3. Add the garlic and cook for 2 more minutes then stir in the mushrooms and rice.
4. When they are well coated with the oil, add 2 ladles of the hot stock.
5. Cook, stirring occasionally, until most of the stock has been absorbed before adding the next 2 ladles.
6. Continue in this way for around 15 minutes or until the rice is just tender.
7. Stir in the butter, then cover the pan and take off the heat to rest for 4 minutes.
8. Uncover the pan and season well with salt and pepper, then spoon into warm bowls.

SERVES: **4** | PREP TIME: **5 MINS** | COOKING TIME: **10 MINS**

Vegetable Fajitas

3 tbsp olive oil
1 red pepper, chopped
1 green pepper, chopped
1 yellow pepper, chopped
½ aubergine (eggplant), cubed
100 g / 3 ½ oz / 1 ¼ cup button mushrooms, thickly sliced
2 tbsp fajita seasoning mix
8 soft flour tortillas

1. Heat the oil in a large sauté pan and stir-fry the vegetables for 8 minutes or until starting to soften.
2. Sprinkle over the seasoning mix and cook for 2 more minutes then divide the mixture between the tortillas, roll up and serve.

SERVES: **1** | PREP TIME: **2 MINS** | COOKING TIME: **4 MINS**

White Asparagus Omelette

3 large eggs
10 g butter
1 tbsp flat leaf parsley, finely chopped
75 g / 2 ½ oz / ¾ cup canned white asparagus, drained

1. Break the eggs into a jug with a pinch of salt and pepper and beat them gently to break up the yolks.
2. Heat the butter in a non-stick frying pan until sizzling then pour in the eggs.
3. Cook over a medium heat until the eggs start to set around the outside. Use a spatula to draw the sides of the omelette into the centre and tilt the pan to fill the gaps with more liquid egg.
4. Sprinkle with parsley and arrange the asparagus on top then continue cooking until the top of the omelette is just set.
5. Shake the omelette out onto a plate, folding it over as you go.

Fried Eggs with Asparagus and Mushrooms

200 g / 7 oz / 2 cups / 2 cups fresh
  asparagus
2 eggs
1 mushroom, sliced
2 tbsp olive oil

1. Snap the woody ends off the asparagus and cut the spears in half.
2. Steam the asparagus for 5 minutes or until tender.
3. Heat the olive oil in a large sauté pan and add the eggs. Fry for 2-3 minutes until they start to bubble, then add the sliced mushroom and asparagus to the pan and allow to cook for another 2-3 minutes.
4. Once the eggs are fully fried, use a spatula to remove them from the pan and arrange with the asparagus and mushroom on a plate.
5. Season to taste and serve immediately.

Aubergine and Courgettes with Walnuts

4 tbsp olive oil
1 onion, finely chopped
1 aubergine (eggplant), finely chopped
2 courgettes (zucchini), finely chopped
1 clove garlic, crushed
100 g / 3 ½ oz / ¾ cup walnuts, chopped
2 tbsp flat leaf parsley, chopped

1. Heat the olive oil in a large sauté pan and fry the onion, aubergine and courgette with a pinch of salt for 25 minutes, stirring occasionally.
2. When any liquid that comes out of the vegetables has evaporated and they start to turn golden, add the garlic and cook for 2 more minutes.
3. Stir in the walnuts and parsley then season to taste with salt and pepper.

SERVES: 1 | PREP TIME: 5-10 MINS | COOKING TIME: 15-20 MINS

Wild Mushroom Omelette

200 g / 8 oz / 2 cups mixed wild
   mushrooms
1 tbsp olive oil
4 tbsp butter
3 large eggs
1 tbsp chives, chopped

1. Pick over the mushrooms and brush
   away any soil with a pastry brush.
   Cut the bigger mushrooms into
   bite-sized pieces.
2. Heat the olive oil and half the
   butter in a large sauté pan
   until sizzling.
3. Add the mushrooms, season
   with salt and pepper and cook for
   10 minutes, stirring occasionally.
4. Break the eggs into a jug with a
   pinch of salt and pepper and beat
   them gently to break up the yolks.
5. Heat the rest of the butter in a
   non-stick frying pan until sizzling
   then pour in the eggs.
6. Cook over a medium heat until
   the eggs start to set around the
   outside. Use a spatula to draw the
   sides of the omelette into the
   centre and tilt the pan to fill the
   gaps with more liquid egg.
7. Repeat the process until the top
   of the omelette is just set then fold
   it over and slide onto a warm plate.
8. Spoon over the mushrooms and
   sprinkle with chives.

SERVES: **4** | PREP TIME: **2 MINS** | COOKING TIME: **40-45 MINS**

Roasted Vegetable Crustless Quiche

1 courgette (zucchini), cut into chunks
1 aubergine (eggplant) , cut into chunks
1 red pepper, cut into chunks
1 yellow pepper, cut into chunks
2 tbsp olive oil
6 eggs
1 tbsp basil, finely shredded

1. Preheat the oven to 180°C (160° fan), 355 F, gas 4.
2. Rub the vegetables with oil and season with salt and pepper then roast
   for 20 minutes.
3. Lightly beat the eggs and stir in the vegetables.
4. Pour the mixture into a small baking dish and bake in the oven for
   20–25 minutes or until just set in the centre.
5. Sprinkle with basil and serve warm or at room temperature.

Light Bites

Asparagus and Parmesan Salad

200 g / 7 oz / 2 cups / 1 cup asparagus, trimmed
100 g / 3 ½ oz / 2 cups mixed salad leaves
100 g / 3 ½ oz / ⅔ cup cherry tomatoes, quartered
8 baby spring onions (scallions), halved lengthways
75 g / 2 ½ oz / ½ cup kalamata olives
2 tbsp sesame seeds
30 g / 1 oz / ⅕ Parmesan

FOR THE DRESSING
1 tbsp mayonnaise
1 tbsp natural yogurt

1 tbsp lemon juice
1 tsp fresh thyme leaves, chopped

1. Blanch the asparagus in boiling salted water for 6 minutes or until al dente. Plunge into cold water and drain well.
2. Divide the leaves between 4 plates and top with the asparagus, tomatoes, onions and olives.
3. Sprinkle over the sesame seeds and shave over some Parmesan.
4. Mix the dressing ingredients together and drizzle over the salad.

Cheese Goujons

400 g / 14 oz / 3 ½ cups Emmental or young Gouda
4 tbsp plain (all-purpose) flour
1 egg, beaten
75 g / 2 ½ oz / ½ cup panko breadcrumbs
2–3 litres / 3 ½ pints–5 pints / 8–12 cups sunflower oil

1. Cut the cheese into fingers with a sharp knife.
2. Put the flour, egg and panko breadcrumbs in 3 separate bowls.
3. Dip the cheese first in the flour, then in egg, then in the breadcrumbs.
4. Heat the oil in a deep fat fryer, according to the manufacturer's instructions, to a temperature of 180°C.
5. Lower the goujons in the fryer basket and cook for 4–5 minutes or until crisp and golden brown.
6. Line a large bowl with a thick layer of kitchen paper and when they are ready, tip them into the bowl to remove any excess oil.
7. Sprinkle with a little sea salt to taste and serve immediately.

SERVES: **4-6** | PREP TIME: **5 MINS** | COOKING TIME: **30 MINS**

Caponata with Boiled Eggs

100 ml / 3 ½ fl. oz / ½ cup olive oil
1 aubergine (eggplant), diced
2 sticks celery, diced
2 red peppers, diced
1 onion, finely chopped
1 red chilli (chili), finely chopped
3 tbsp red wine vinegar
3 tomatoes, finely chopped
50 g / 1 ¾ oz / ⅓ cup black olives
1 hard-boiled egg, quartered

1. Heat the oil in a large sauté pan and cook the aubergine until golden brown.
   Remove from the pan with a slotted spoon and leave to drain in a sieve.
2. Fry the celery in the same way and leave to drain with the aubergine, followed
   by the peppers.
3. Fry the onion and chilli for 5 minutes or until starting to caramelise then
   add the red wine vinegar and bubble away almost to nothing.
4. Add the tomatoes to the pan with their juice and cook for 5 minutes.
5. Return the fried vegetables to the pan and simmer together for another
   5 minutes. Season to taste with salt and black pepper.
6. Spoon the caponata into a serving dish and top with the olives and egg
   quarters. Serve warm or at room temperature.

Almond and Olive Tapenade Crostini

2 tbsp blanched almonds
100 g / 3 ½ oz / ⅔ cup green olives, pitted
3 tbsp capers
1 clove garlic, crushed
2 tbsp mint leaves, torn
2 tbsp olive oil
2 slices white bread, halved diagonally
sun-dried tomatoes and basil, to serve

1. Put the almonds, olives and capers on a chopping board and chop them all together until coarsely chopped and evenly mixed.
2. Scrape the mixture into a bowl and stir in the garlic, mint and oil then season to taste with salt and pepper.
3. Toast the bread then spread the tapenade on top.
4. Serve with some sun-dried tomatoes and basil on the side.

Baked Tomatoes with Parsley

4 beefsteak or marmande tomatoes
50 g / 1 ¾ oz / ⅔ cup breadcrumbs
50 g / 1 ¾ oz / ½ cup Parmesan, grated
1 clove of garlic, crushed
4 tbsp flat leaf parsley, roughly chopped
4 tbsp olive oil

1. Preheat the oven to 200°C (180° fan), 390 F, gas 6.
2. Cut the tops off the tomatoes and scoop out a 1 cm layer of the inside.
3. Mix the breadcrumbs and Parmesan with the garlic and parsley and a good grind of black pepper, then pack the mixture into the tomato cavities.
4. Arrange the tomatoes in a baking dish and drizzle over the oil.
5. Bake for 25 minutes or until the topping is golden and the tomatoes are soft, but not collapsing.
6. Serve with plenty of crusty bread to mop up the juices.

Salade Niçoise

400 g / 14 oz / 2 ⅔ cup charlotte
  potatoes, halved

1 oak leaf lettuce, leaves separated

1 jar white tuna in olive oil,
  drained and cubed

6 tomatoes, quartered

75 g / 2 ½ oz / ½ cup black olives,
  pitted

4 tbsp extra virgin olive oil

a few sprigs chervil to garnish

1. Boil the potatoes in salted water
   for 12 minutes or until tender,
   then drain well.
2. Arrange the lettuce on four
   serving plates and arrange the
   tuna, potatoes, tomatoes and
   olives on top.
3. Drizzle with olive oil and garnish
   with chervil.

Spinach and Walnut Bruschetta

100 g / 3 ½ oz / 1 ⅓ cups baby leaf spinach

4 slices walnut bread

1 clove garlic, halved

2 tbsp walnut oil

50 g / 1 ¾ oz / ⅓ cup goats' cheese, cubed

2 tbsp walnuts, roughly chopped

1. Heat a saucepan on the hob and wash the spinach, then put it in the pan and cover with a lid.
2. Let it steam for 2 minutes, then tip it into a sieve to drain off any excess liquid.
3. Toast the walnut bread then rub with the halved garlic clove and drizzle with the walnut oil.
4. Arrange the hot spinach on top and dot over the cubed goats' cheese and roughly chopped walnuts.

Roast Chicken and Boiled Egg Salad

a small bunch of radishes, trimmed
1 lettuce, separated into leaves
½ cucumber, sliced
2 tomatoes, cut into wedges
1 stick celery, chopped
2 hard-boiled eggs, quartered
75 g / 3 oz / ½ cup black olives, pitted
2 skin-on roasted chicken breasts, sliced
mayonnaise, to serve

1. Slit the ends of the radishes and put them in a bowl of iced water for 5 minutes to fan out.
2. Line a large serving bowl with lettuce leaves and arrange the cucumber, tomato and celery on top.
3. Add a ring of boiled egg quarters and radishes round the outside and put the chicken in the middle.
4. Scatter over the olives and serve with a bowl of mayonnaise on the side.

SERVES: **4** | PREP TIME: **5 MINS** | COOKING TIME: **40-45 MINS**

Potato Wedges with Thyme

4 tbsp olive oil
800 g / 1 lb 12 oz / 6 cup Maris Piper potatoes, cut into wedges
2 tbsp fresh thyme leaves

1. Preheat the oven to 220°C (200° fan), 430 F, gas 7.
2. Put the oil in a large roasting tin and heat in the oven for 5 minutes.
3. Carefully tip the potato wedges into the pan and turn to coat in the oil,
   then sprinkle with thyme leaves and season well with salt and black pepper.
4. Bake the wedges for 40–45 minutes, turning them every 15 minutes.

Deep-fried Mozzarella

4 tbsp plain (all-purpose) flour
1 egg, beaten
75 g / 2 ½ oz / ½ cup panko
   breadcrumbs
4 mozzarella balls, sliced
2–3 litres / 3 ½ pints–5 pints /
   8–12 cups sunflower oil
rocket (arugula) leaves to serve

1. Put the flour, egg and panko breadcrumbs in 3 separate bowls.
2. Dip the mozzarella in the flour, then the egg, then the breadcrumbs, making sure it is well coated.
3. Heat the oil in a deep fat fryer, according to the manufacturer's instructions, to a temperature of 180°C.
4. Lower the mozzarella slices in the fryer basket and cook for 4–5 minutes or until crisp and golden brown.
5. Line a large bowl with a thick layer of kitchen paper and when they are ready, tip them into the bowl to remove any excess oil.
6. Sprinkle with a little sea salt to taste and serve immediately on a bed of rocket.

SERVES: **4** | PREP TIME: **2 MINS** | COOKING TIME: **20 MINS**

Curry-fried Potatoes

800 g / 1 lb 12 oz / 5 ⅓ cup charlotte
 potatoes, peeled and sliced
4 tbsp olive oil
1 onion, sliced
3 tsp mild curry powder
lime slices and coriander (cilantro)
 leaves, to garnish

1. Boil the potatoes in salted water for
 8 minutes then drain well and leave
 to steam dry for 2 minutes.
2. Heat the oil in a large sauté pan
 and fry the onion for 4 minutes.
3. Add the potatoes and curry
 powder and stir-fry for 4 minutes or
 until golden.
4. Transfer to a hot serving plate and
 garnish with lime and coriander.

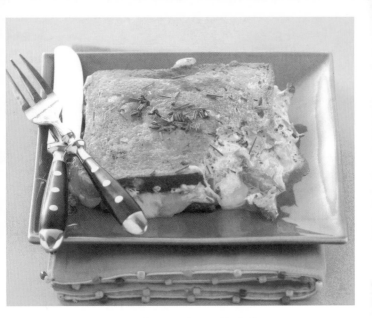

SERVES: **2** | PREP TIME: **2 MINS** | COOKING TIME: **20 MINS**

Cheese, Tomato and Mustard Sandwich

2 tbsp butter, softened
4 slices white bread
150 g / 5 ½ oz / 1 cup Reblochon cheese
1 medium tomato, thinly sliced
3 tbsp crème fraiche
2 tsp wholegrain mustard
2 tsp chives, chopped

1. Preheat a sandwich press.
2. Butter the bread on both sides and top two of the pieces with the cheese and tomato slices.
3. Mix the crème fraiche with the mustard and chives and spread it over the other two slices, then close the sandwiches and transfer them to the sandwich press.
4. Toast the sandwiches for 4 minutes or until the bread is golden and the cheese has melted inside.

SERVES: **4** | PREP TIME: **5 MINS** | COOKING TIME: **25 MINS**

Spring Vegetable Soup

2 tbsp olive oil
1 onion, finely chopped
2 cloves garlic, crushed
4 small new potatoes, quartered
100 g / 3 ½ oz / 1 cup asparagus
  spears, chopped
100 g / 3 ½ oz / 1 cup mange tout
  (snow peas), chopped

100 g / 3 ½ oz / 1 cup cabbage,
  shredded
100 g / 3 ½ oz / ⅔ cup fresh peas
1 litre / 1 pint 16 fl. oz / 4 cups
  vegetable stock
2 tbsp crème fraiche
2 tbsp flat leaf parsley, chopped
lemon wedges, to serve

1. Heat the oil in a saucepan and fry the onion for 5 minutes or until softened.
   Add the garlic and cook for 2 more minutes then stir in the vegetables.
2. Pour in the vegetable stock and bring to the boil.
3. Simmer for 15 minutes then stir in the crème fraiche and parsley.
4. Try the soup and adjust the seasoning with salt and pepper.
5. Ladle the soup into four warm bowls and serve each one with a lemon
   wedge for squeezing over.

Warm Scotch Eggs

7 small eggs
4 good quality pork sausages
4 tbsp plain (all-purpose) flour
75 g / 2 ½ oz / ½ cup panko
 breadcrumbs
2–3 litres / 3 ½ pints–5 pints /
 8–12 cups sunflower oil

1. Put 6 of the eggs in a pan of cold water then bring to a simmer and cook for 5 minutes.
2. Cool, then peel off the shells.
3. Skin the sausages and divide the meat into 6. Flatten a portion of sausage meat onto your hand and put an egg in the centre, then squeeze the meat round the outside to coat. Repeat with the other 5 eggs.
4. Put the flour, remaining egg and panko breadcrumbs in three separate bowls.
5. Dip the scotch eggs first in the flour, then in egg, then in the breadcrumbs.
6. Heat the oil in a deep fat fryer, according to the manufacturer's instructions, to a temperature of 180°C.
7. Lower the scotch eggs in the fryer basket and cook for 4–5 minutes or until crisp and golden brown.
8. Sprinkle with a little sea salt and serve immediately.

SERVES: **4** | PREP TIME: **4 MINS** | COOKING TIME: **15 MINS**

Stuffed Mushrooms

8 anchovy fillets
100 g / 3 ½ oz / ⅔ cup mascarpone
1 clove garlic, crushed
1 tbsp chives, chopped
1 tbsp flat leaf parsley, chopped
4 large mushrooms, destalked

1. Preheat the oven to 200°C (180° fan), 390 F, gas 6.
2. Finely chop 4 of the anchovy fillets and mix them with the mascarpone, garlic and half the herbs.
3. Divide the mixture between the mushroom cavities and top each one with a whole anchovy fillet and some more herbs.
4. Spread the mushrooms out on a baking tray and bake for 15 minutes or until the mushroom has softened and the topping is golden brown and bubbling.

Feta and Cherry Tomato Salad

6 large lettuce leaves
100 g / 3 ½ oz / ⅔ cup feta, cubed
6 cherry tomatoes, quartered
a few kalamata olives
4 tbsp extra virgin olive oil
½ tsp pink peppercorns, crushed

1. Arrange the lettuce leaves on two plates.
2. Top with the feta, tomatoes and olives.
3. Drizzle with olive oil and sprinkle with pink peppercorns.

Mini Herb Frittatas

6 eggs
½ red onion, finely chopped
2 tbsp flat leaf parsley, finely chopped
2 tbsp chives, finely chopped
2 tbsp basil, finely chopped

1. Preheat the oven to 180°C (160° fan), 355 F, gas 4.
2. Lightly beat the eggs and mix them with the onion and herbs, then season well with salt and pepper.
3. Pour the mixture into a 12-hole silicone cupcake mould and bake in the oven for 15–20 minutes or until the frittatas are set in the centre.
4. Serve warm or at room temperature.

SERVES: 4 | PREP TIME: 5 MINS | COOKING TIME: 40 MINS

Potato Wedges and Sprouts with Bacon

4 tbsp olive oil

800 g / 1 lb 12 oz / 4 ½ cup Maris Piper potatoes, cut into wedges

400 g / 14 oz / 4 cups Brussels sprouts, trimmed

200 g / 7 oz / 2 cups streaky bacon

1. Preheat the oven to 220°C (200° fan), 430 F, gas 7.
2. Put the oil in a large roasting tin and heat in the oven for 5 minutes.
3. Carefully tip the potato wedges into the pan and turn to coat in the oil, then sprinkle with a little salt and pepper and bake for 15 minutes.
4. Meanwhile, wrap the sprouts in bacon and secure with cocktails sticks.
5. When the 15 minutes are up, add the sprouts to the pan and stir to coat in the oil.
6. Roast for another 25 minutes or until the sprouts and potatoes are cooked through.

SERVES: **2** | PREP TIME: **5 MINS** | COOKING TIME: **25 MINS**

Pesto Risotto

1 litre / 1 pint 15 fl. oz / 4 cups good quality vegetable stock
2 tbsp olive oil
1 onion, finely chopped
2 cloves of garlic, crushed
150 g / 5 ½ oz / ¾ cup risotto rice
100 g / 3 ½ oz / ½ cup pesto
50 g / 1 ¾ oz / ½ cup Parmesan, finely grated
a handful of rocket (arugula) leaves

1. Heat the stock in a saucepan.
2. Heat the olive oil in a sauté pan and gently fry the onion for 5 minutes without colouring.
3. Add the garlic and cook for 2 more minutes then stir in the rice.
4. When it is well coated with the oil, add 2 ladles of the hot stock.
5. Cook, stirring occasionally, until most of the stock has been absorbed before adding the next 2 ladles.
6. Continue in this way for around 15 minutes or until the rice is just tender.
7. Stir in the pesto and Parmesan, then cover the pan and take off the heat to rest for 4 minutes.
8. Uncover the pan and season well with salt and pepper, then spoon into warm bowls.
9. Garnish with rocket leaves and serve immediately.

SERVES: 4 | PREP TIME: 5 MINS | COOKING TIME: 40 MINS

French Onion Soup

2 tbsp olive oil
3 onions, sliced
2 cloves garlic, crushed
1 litre / 1 pint 16 fl. oz / 4 cups
  vegetable stock

FOR THE CROUTES
1 baguette, sliced
100 g / 3 ½ oz / 1 cup Gruyère, grated

1. Heat the oil in a saucepan and fry the onions for 20 minutes. Add the garlic and cook for 2 more minutes then stir in the vegetable stock and bring to the boil.
2. Simmer for 15 minutes then taste the soup and adjust the seasoning with salt and pepper.
3. Meanwhile, preheat the grill to its highest setting.
4. Toast the baguette slices on one side under the grill then turn them over and sprinkle with cheese.
5. Grill the other side until the cheese is golden and bubbling.
6. Ladle the soup into four warm bowls and float the croutes on top.

MAKES: **20-24** | PREP TIME: **25 MINS** | COOKING TIME: **12-15 MINS**

Goats' Cheese Samosas

200 g / 7 oz / 2 cups / 1 ¼ cup fresh goats' cheese
1 clove garlic, crushed
1 lemon, zest finely grated
2 tbsp flat leaf parsley, chopped
225 g / 8 oz filo pastry
100 g / 3 ½ oz / ½ cup butter, melted
baby leaf spinach, to serve

1. Preheat the oven to 180°C (160° fan), 355 F, gas 4 and grease a large baking tray.
2. Mash the goats' cheese with the garlic, lemon zest and parsley and season with salt and pepper.
3. Cut the pile of filo sheets in half then take one halved sheet and brush it with melted butter.
4. Arrange a heaped teaspoon of goats' cheese at one end then fold the corner across and triangle-fold it into a samosa shape.
5. Transfer the samosa to the baking tray and repeat with the rest of the filo and goats' cheese.
6. Bake the samosas for 12–15 minutes or until the filo is crisp and golden brown.
7. Serve on a bed of spinach.

SERVES: 4 | PREP TIME: 15 MINS | COOKING TIME: 8 MINS

Goats' Cheese Potato Cakes

300 g / 10 ½ oz / 2 cups left over boiled potatoes, cold

1 egg yolk

100 g / 3 ½ oz / ⅔ cup fresh goats' cheese, cubed

2 tbsp fresh chives, chopped

1 tbsp flat leaf parsley, chopped

50 g / 1 ¾ oz / ⅓ cup panko breadcrumbs

4 tbsp olive oil

TO SERVE

1 beefsteak tomato

28 g / 1 oz rocket (arugula) leaves

a few sprigs parsley and chives

1 tbsp olive oil

1. Mash the potato with the egg yolk and plenty of salt and pepper then knead in the goats' cheese and herbs.
2. Divide the mixture into 4 and shape it into patties. Dip the potato cakes in the breadcrumbs to coat.
3. Heat the oil in a large frying pan and fry the potato cakes for 4 minutes on each side or until golden brown.
4. Meanwhile, cut 4 large slices from the middle of the tomato and cut the ends into cubes.
5. Put a tomato slice in the centre of each plate and arrange the rocket, cubed tomato and herbs round the outside.
6. Drizzle the salad with oil then position a potato cake on top of each tomato slice.

SERVES: **4** | PREP TIME: **5 MINS** | COOKING TIME: **30 MINS**

Leek, Potato and Parsley Soup

2 tbsp olive oil
2 tbsp butter
3 leeks, julienned
2 cloves garlic, crushed
2 Maris Piper potatoes, peeled and cubed
1 litre / 1 pint 16 fl. oz / 4 cups vegetable stock
2 tbsp crème fraiche
a small bunch of parsley, chopped

1. Heat the oil and butter in a saucepan and fry the leeks for 8 minutes or until softened.
2. Remove a spoonful of the leeks from the pan and reserve for a garnish.
3. Add the garlic and potatoes to the pan and cook for 2 more minutes, then stir in the vegetable stock and bring to the boil.
4. Simmer for 15 minutes then stir in the crème fraiche and parsley.
5. Blend the soup until smooth with a liquidizer or immersion blender.
6. Try the soup and adjust the seasoning with salt and pepper.
7. Ladle the soup into 4 warm bowls and top each one with a few strands of fried leek.

Vegetable Soup

2 tbsp olive oil
1 onion, finely chopped
2 cloves garlic, crushed
4 small new potatoes, quartered
100 g / 3 ½ oz / ¾ cup carrots,
    finely chopped
100 g / 3 ½ oz / ⅔ cup sweetcorn
100 g / 3 ½ oz / ⅔ cup fresh peas
600 ml / 1 pint vegetable stock
400 g / 14 oz / 2 ½ cup canned
    tomatoes, chopped

1. Heat the oil in a saucepan and fry the onion for 5 minutes or until softened. Add the garlic and cook for 2 more minutes then stir in the vegetables.
2. Pour in the vegetable stock and tomatoes and bring to the boil.
3. Simmer for 15 minutes then ladle half of the soup into a liquidizer and blend until smooth.
4. Return the blended soup to the pan, stir well and season with a little salt and pepper.

Stuffed Courgettes

4 courgettes (zucchini)
6 good quality pork sausages, skinned
2 tbsp crème fraiche
1 tsp lemon zest, finely grated
2 tbsp flat leaf parsley, chopped

1. Preheat the oven to 220°C (200° fan), 430 F, gas 7.
2. Cut the courgettes in half and use a melon baller to scoop out the middles.
3. Mix the sausage meat with the crème fraiche, lemon zest and parsley, then spoon it into the courgette cavities.
4. Arrange the courgettes in a roasting tin and bake in the oven for 30 minutes or until golden brown and cooked through.

SERVES: 2 | PREP TIME: **2 MINS** | COOKING TIME: **10 MINS**

Chicken and Asparagus Salad

2 large skinless chicken breasts
2 slices sourdough bread
6 tbsp olive oil
1 tbsp sherry vinegar
6 asparagus spears
½ small red onion, sliced
small bunch of young radish leaves

1. Preheat a large griddle pan until smoking hot.
2. Brush the chicken and sourdough with oil and season with salt and pepper.
3. Cook the chicken for 4 minutes on each side or until cooked through but still juicy.
4. Boil the asparagus in salted water for 4 minutes or until al dente, then slice each spear in half lengthways.
5. Griddle the sourdough for 1 minute on each side or until nicely toasted.
6. Cut it into quarters and put in the bottom of 2 bowls.
7. Mix the rest of the oil with the vinegar and a little salt and pepper to make a dressing.
8. Toss the asparagus, onion and radish leaves with the dressing and arrange on top of the toasted sourdough.
9. Cut each chicken breast into 3 pieces and position on top of the salad.

SERVES: **4** | PREP TIME: **5 MINS**

Sun-dried Tomato and Prosciutto Salad

12 thin slices prosciutto
1 jar sun-dried tomatoes in oil,
  drained, oil reserved
1 yellow pepper, cubed
1 ball mozzarella, cubed
50 g / 1 ¾ oz / ⅓ cup kalamata
  olives, pitted
50 g / 1 ¾ oz / 1 cup rocket
  (arugula) leaves

2 tbsp toasted pine nuts
a small bunch basil, torn

FOR THE DRESSING
2 tbsp oil from the tomato jar
½ lemon, juiced

1. Toss together all of the salad ingredients and divide between four plates.
2. Whisk the oil and lemon juice together and drizzle over the salad.

Stuffed Vine Tomatoes

4 tomato vines
200 g / 7 oz / 2 cups / 1 cup cream
  cheese
4 tbsp chives, chopped
75 g / 2 ½ oz / ½ cup smoked
  salmon, chopped
75 g / 2 ½ oz / ½ cup cooked
  ham, chopped
salt and pepper

1. Cut the tops off the tomatoes and scoop out and discard the seeds.
2. Mix the cream cheese with the chives and season with salt and pepper, then divide it into two separate bowls.
3. Add the salmon to one and the ham to the other then use the mixture to stuff the tomatoes.
4. Transfer to a serving plate and serve immediately.

Gorgonzola and Tomato Toasts

8 slices sourdough bread
8 slices Gorgonzola
8 cherry tomatoes
olive oil, to drizzle

1. Preheat the grill to its highest setting.
2. Toast the slices of sourdough on one side under the grill.
3. Turn them over and top each one with a slice of Gorgonzola, a tomato and a drizzle of olive oil.
4. Grill for 3 more minutes or until the tomato is soft and the bread is toasted at the edges.
5. Serve 2 toasts per person.

Index